MW00679736

This book is a gift to:

_____

Message:

_____

_____

_____

_____

_____

From:

_____

Blessings of Hope

© 2013 Christian Art Gifts, RSA
        Christian Art Gifts Inc., IL, USA

        Art © Bethany Berndt-Shackelford, licensed by Suzanne Cruise

Designed by Christian Art Gifts

Scripture quotations are taken from the *Holy Bible*, New International Version® NIV®. Copyright © 1973, 1978, 1984, 2011 by International Bible Society. Used by permission of Zondervan Publishing House. All rights reserved.

Scripture quotations are taken from the *Holy Bible*, New Living Translation®, second edition. Copyright © 1996, 2004, 2007 by Tyndale House Publishers, Inc., Carol Stream, Illinois 60188. All rights reserved.

Scripture quotations are taken from the New King James Version. Copyright © 1979, 1980, 1982 by Thomas Nelson, Inc. Used by permission. All rights reserved.

Scripture quotations are taken from the *Holy Bible*, English Standard Version. Copyright © 2001 by Crossway Bibles, a division of Good News Publishers. Used by permission. All rights reserved.

Printed in China

ISBN 978-1-4321-0734-5

Christian Art Gifts has made every effort to trace the ownership of all quotes and poems in this book. In the event of any question that may arise from the use of any quote or poem, we regret any error made and will be pleased to make the necessary correction in future editions of this book.

© All rights reserved. No part of this book may be reproduced in any form without permission in writing from the publisher, except in the case of brief quotations embodied in critical articles or reviews.

13   14   15   16   17   18   19   20   21   22   –   10   9   8   7   6   5   4   3   2   1

Blessings

of

HOPE

MESSAGES

of Assurance & Truth

christian
art gifts ®

BE

STRONG

and take heart, all you who

HOPE

in the Lord.

[Ps. 31:24]

God is the **ONLY ONE** who can make the valley of trouble a **DOOR OF HOPE.**

Catherine Marshall

BE JOYFUL IN

HOPE

patient in affliction,
faithful in

PRAYER.

{ROM. 12:12}

He that lives in **HOPE**

danceth without **MUSIC**.

Geoorge Herbert

WE HAVE THIS HOPE AS AN

ANCHOR

for the soul,

FIRM & SECURE.

[Heb. 6:19]

Cast your **CARES** on God;

that **ANCHOR HOLDS.**

Frank Moore Colby

THE LORD

is good to those
WHOSE HOPE is in Him,
to the

one

 who seeks
HIM.

Lam. 3:25

God **ALWAYS** gives His best to those

who leave the **CHOICE** with **HIM**.

Jim Elliot

May the God of

HOPE

fill you with all

 JOY & PEACE

in believing, that you may abound
in hope by the power of the

Holy Spirit.

[Rom. 15:13]

HOPE fills the afflicted soul with

such inward JOY and consolation,

that it can LAUGH

while tears are in the eye,

sigh and sing all in a BREATH.

WILLIAM GURNALL

"I KNOW THE PLANS I HAVE FOR YOU ...

PLANS

& to prosper you
and not to harm you,
plans to give you

hope

AND A FUTURE."

{Jer. 29:11}

God gives us **HOPES** and **DREAMS** for certain things to **HAPPEN** in our lives, but He doesn't always allow us to see the exact timing of **HIS PLAN**.

JOYCE MEYER

Those who

hope in the **LORD** will renew

their strength.

They will soar on

wings

like eagles; they will run and not
grow weary, they will walk

& NOT BE FAINT.

Isa. 40:31

Everything that was

WRITTEN IN THE PAST

was **written** to teach us, so that through endurance

& THE ENCOURAGEMENT OF THE SCRIPTURES

we might have

HOPE.

{ROM. 15:4}

The **WINGS** of **HOPE** carry

us, soaring **HIGH** above

the driving winds of life.

Ana Jacob

The word hope I take for **FAITH**;

and indeed hope is nothing else but the

CONSTANCY of **FAITH**.

John Calvin

Faith has to do with **THINGS** that are **NOT SEEN** and hope with things that are **NOT AT HAND**.

Thomas Aquinas

Faith

is the assurance of things

HOPED FOR

the **conviction** of
things **not seen.**

{HEB. 11:1}

JOYFUL

are those **whose**

hope

is in the Lord

their God.

{Ps. 146:5}

Only in the darkness

can you see the **STARS**.

MARTIN LUTHER KING, JR.

If you have been **REDUCED** to

GOD being your **ONLY HOPE**,

you are in a **GOOD** place.

JIM LAFFOON

23

We also rejoice in our

SUFFERINGS

because we **know** that

suffering produces

perseverance

PERSEVERANCE produces
CHARACTER
& character produces

hope.

[Rom. 5:3-4]

I WAIT FOR

THE LORD

my soul waits, and in

His Word

I put my **hope.**

{Ps. 130:5}

26

Do not **LOOK** to your hope,
but to **CHRIST**,
the source of your **HOPE**.

CHARLES H. SPURGEON

The **SAFEST** place in all the world is in the will of God, and the safest **PROTECTION** in all **THE WORLD** is the name of God.

WARREN WIERSBE

You will be

SECURE

because there is *hope*;
you will look about you

and take your rest in

safety.

[Job 11:18]

GOD

will never forget the
🌿**needy**;
the hope of the afflicted
WILL NEVER
perish.

{Ps. 9:18}

If you feel like you're at the end of your

ROPE, tie a knot and **HANG ON!**

Because God's a **GOD OF MIRACLES,**

and He's holding the other end.

PAT HICKS

Without CHRIST
there is NO HOPE.

CHARLES H. SPURGEON

WHEN DOUBTS

filled my mind,

YOUR COMFORT

gave me renewed

HOPE & CHEER.

{Ps. 94:19}

Hope does not

DISAPPOINT US

because God has poured
out **His love** into our
hearts by the

Holy Spirit,

whom **He** has given us.

{ROM. 5:5}

We must **ACCEPT** finite disappointment,
but never lose **INFINITE** hope.

MARTIN LUTHER KING, JR.

BLESSED

IS THE ONE WHO

trusts

in the Lord, whose

CONFIDENCE

IS IN HIM.

{Jer. 17:7}

POSITIVE MINDS full of FAITH
and HOPE produce positive LIVES.

JOYCE MEYER

Other men see only a hopeless end,

but the Christian **REJOICES**

in an **ENDLESS** hope.

GILBERT M. BEEKEN

THEREFORE,

with minds that are alert

& fully sober,

set your hope on the

grace

to be brought to you
when Jesus Christ is revealed
AT HIS COMING.

{1 Pet. 1:13}

When **GOD** comes down,

He removes the immovable difficulties.

When God comes down, the impossible

becomes **REALITY**. God moves on

behalf of the **ONE** who waits.

ANONYMOUS

Hope
IN THE LORD!

For with the Lord there is

STEADFAST
LOVE

and with Him is

plentiful redemption.

{Ps. 130:7}

Therefore my heart is

glad

and my tongue
REJOICES

my body also
will live in

hope.

{ACTS 2:26}

Having been justified by

HIS GRACE

we might become **heirs**

having the hope of

eternal life.

{Titus 3:7}

HOPE is the thing with feathers

that perches in the **SOUL**, and

SINGS the tune without words,

and never stops at all.

MARTIN LUTHER

AND NOW

these three remain:

faith, **HOPE**

& *love.*

{1 COR. 13:13}

Our **HOPE** lies in **BELIEVING**

in God's **LOVE** for our lives.

Anonymous

To live without **HOPE** is to

cease to live.

Fyodor Dostoevsky

There is

SURELY

a **future** hope for you,

and your **hope**

WILL NOT

be cut off